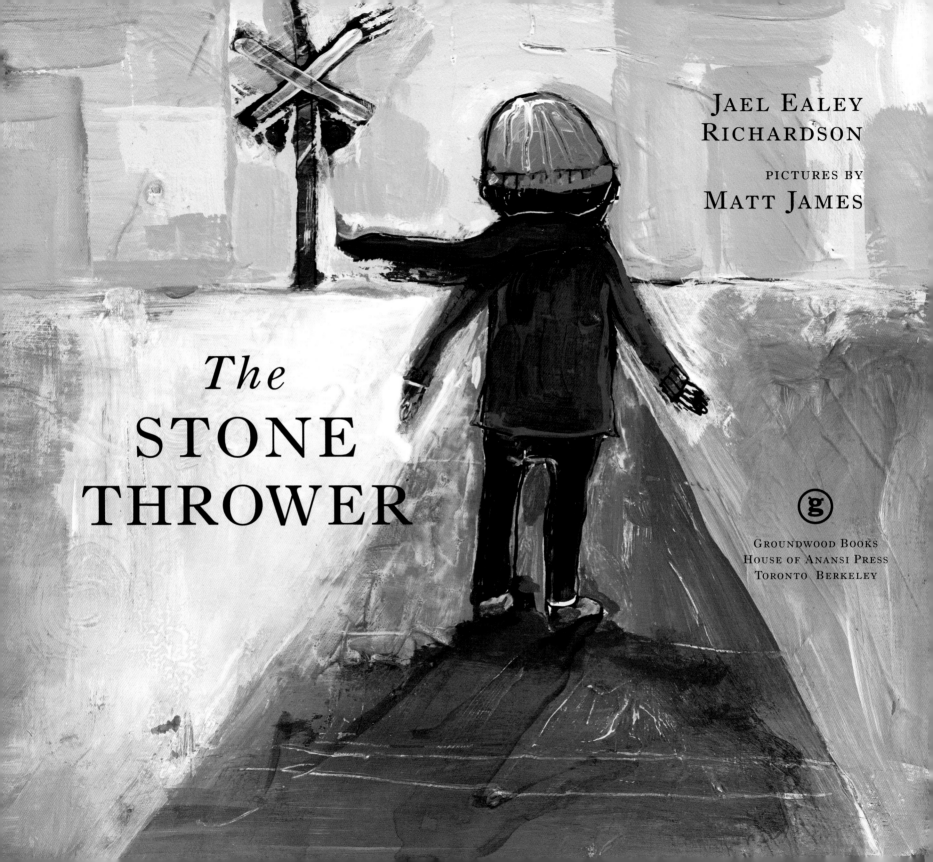

JAEL EALEY
RICHARDSON

PICTURES BY
MATT JAMES

The
STONE
THROWER

GROUNDWOOD BOOKS
HOUSE OF ANANSI PRESS
TORONTO BERKELEY

THIS IS A STORY that happened a long time ago in a place that's far away (unless of course you happen to be from a small town in Ohio called Portsmouth). It's a story about a kid who lived in hard times, a kid who had a big dream that seemed almost impossible.

Chuck Ealey was born in Portsmouth, Ohio, in 1950. Back then there were separate schools and separate restrooms and separate neighborhoods for black people, because some Americans didn't believe that all people were equal, regardless of their skin color.

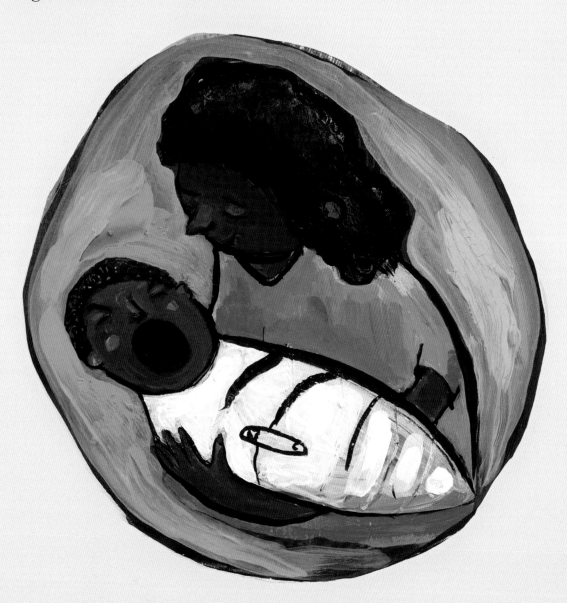

Chuck grew up in the North End, a neighborhood that was separated from the rest of town by a set of long, stony railroad tracks. The buildings in the North End were rundown, and there was nowhere to swim when the weather got hot, because the pool was on the other side of the train tracks.

NO RUNNING

Chuck's mother had dropped out of school when she was
very young. She had to work hard to raise her son all by
herself. She worked long hours, and she was paid very little.

She wanted things to be different for Chuck.

"Those coal trains that come through, they don't stop here," she said. "They don't stop until they get where they're going. I want you to be just like that. Do you remember where you're going, son?"

Chuck smiled at her with a big, broad grin. "I'm going to get out of the North End and get my education."

She smiled and squeezed him tightly.

"That's right," she said.

When Chuck came home from school one day, he felt his tummy rumbling. He couldn't remember the last time he had eaten. The only thing he found in the cupboard was a wheat bar. He chewed and he chomped, but it tasted like twigs. It felt thin and dry in his throat. Worst of all, it still left him hungry.

How could he get out of the North End if they didn't even have enough money for food?

On a crisp fall day, Chuck walked towards the train tracks. He scuffed his shoes against the pavement as the wind whispered gently, as leaves tumbled and danced and cracked beneath his footsteps.

Just then Chuck heard a long, thin whistle in the distance. The ground began to rumble, and the train tracks shook. The stones along the tracks jumped and bounced like hot kernels of popcorn.

Thick, gray clouds huffed and puffed from the smokestacks of a train as it chugged down the railroad tracks towards him.

"CHA-cha-cha-cha. CHA-cha-cha-cha," went the train. "CHA-cha-cha-cha-CHA-cha-cha-cha," it went as the dark coal cars crawled along the tracks like a trail of black ants, each one marked "N & W" for Norfolk & Western.

Suddenly, Chuck had an idea. He selected a stone from the side of the tracks and rubbed it between his fingers. It felt rough, like sandpaper. He tossed it in the air and then caught it.

"Perfect," he said.

As the train charged towards him, Chuck fixed his eyes on the "N" on one of the coal cars. As the train passed and the wind whooshed against him, Chuck pulled back his arm and threw the stone as hard as he could.

Thud!

He missed.

He picked another stone and tried again.

Thud!

As the last car chugged towards him, Chuck narrowed his eyes so he could see the "N" more clearly. He shifted back and forth on his toes. And he waited.

He threw, and watched the stone soar.

BANG!

Chuck smiled and raised his hands in victory.

After that day, Chuck often
went back to the train tracks.
Eventually he learned to throw the
stones just right, so that when the train
was going by and the wind
rushed against him, he could
always hit his target.

At school and at football practice, Chuck did the same thing. When he learned new things and when he had to do the same thing over and over, he thought about standing by the railroad tracks, throwing stones again and again until he got it.

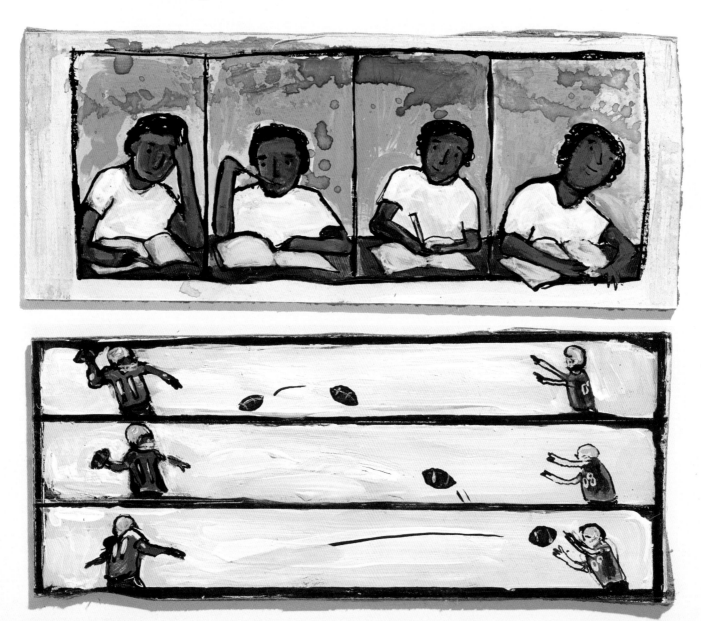

One day his coach asked him to do something important, something that required a kid with determination and focus. Chuck's coach wanted him to play quarterback. He wanted him to throw the ball and lead the team on the field.

Some people didn't think boys like Chuck were smart enough to play quarterback, but Chuck's coach believed in him, and so did his teammates.

But it wasn't easy.

At a game against a rival school, Chuck played a team that was lean and mean. The players called him names, and they ran at him with anger in their eyes and in their hearts.

"Crush him," they cried.

"Get him," they yelled.

With a few seconds left on the scoreboard, Chuck's team was down by five. The team huddled together, heads bent down, arms around each other. They didn't want to lose, but there was only time for one more play.

Chuck got the ball and looked down the field as one of his teammates started to sprint towards the end zone. A player on the opposing team rushed towards Chuck, quick and steady, hungry for the football, hungry for a tackle.

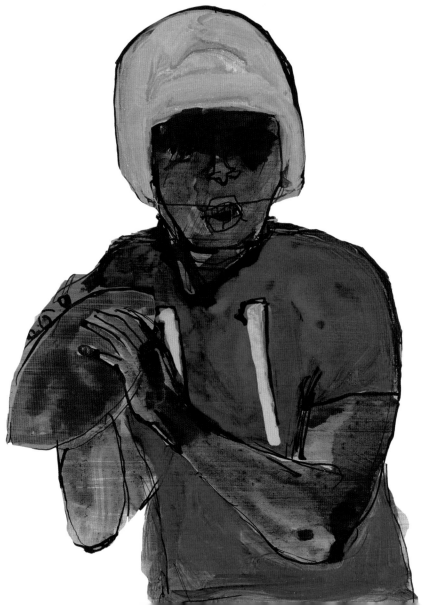

Chuck waited, his feet tiptoeing on the soft grass as the defenceman raced closer and closer.

Chuck thought about those days at the railroad tracks — the rush of the train, the feel of the wind, the rumble of the earth underneath him. He narrowed his eyes so that all he could see was his teammate running faster and faster.

Chuck threw the ball, and it soared through the air. It spiraled down the field, floating, spinning. Everyone waited. Everyone watched as the ball dropped right into the hands of Chuck's teammate as he stepped into the end zone.

Chuck smiled and raised his arms. Touchdown. Victory.

For Earline
JER

CHUCK EALEY won every game as the quarterback at Notre Dame High School. Twenty-seven wins in total. He received a scholarship to the University of Toledo, and he won every game there, too. Thirty-five more wins and a college degree — the best of all his victories. By 1971, he had won more games than any other quarterback in college football history.

It's an unbeatable story that amazes me, even though I've heard it all before, because Chuck Ealey happens to be my father.

But even though he was undefeated, my father would never play professional football in America. The National Football League didn't believe that he could be a great quarterback because of the color of his skin. So my father moved to Canada to play quarterback in the Canadian Football League.

He led the Hamilton Tiger-Cats to the championship, the Grey Cup, in his very first year. He was named the game's Most Valuable Player and the CFL's Rookie of the Year — the best new player in the league. He played for six more years before he retired from the sport that changed his life — and mine — forever.

Text copyright © 2016 by Jael Richardson
Illustrations copyright © 2016 by Matt James
Published in Canada and the USA in 2016 by Groundwood Books

Groundwood Books / House of Anansi Press
groundwoodbooks.com

We acknowledge for their financial support of our publishing program the Canada Council for the Arts, the Ontario Arts Council and the Government of Canada.

Canada Council for the Arts   Conseil des Arts du Canada

ONTARIO ARTS COUNCIL
CONSEIL DES ARTS DE L'ONTARIO
an Ontario government agency
un organisme du gouvernement de l'Ontario

With the participation of the Government of Canada
Avec la participation du gouvernement du Canada   Canada

MIX
Paper from responsible sources
FSC® C012700
www.fsc.org

Library and Archives Canada Cataloguing in Publication
Richardson, Jael Ealey, author
The stone thrower / written by Jael Ealey Richardson ; illustrated by Matt James.
Issued in print and electronic formats.
ISBN 978-1-55498-752-8 (bound). — ISBN 978-1-55498-753-5 (pdf)
1. Ealey, Chuck—Juvenile literature. 2. Football players—Canada—Biography—Juvenile literature. 3. Canadian Football League—History—Juvenile literature. 4. Black Canadians—Biography—Juvenile literature. 5. Richardson, Jael Ealey—Family—Juvenile literature. 6. Fathers and daughters—Canada—Biography—Juvenile literature. I. James, Matt, illustrator II. Title.
GV939.E24R54 2016   j796.335092   C2015-903782-4
C2015-903783-2

The illustrations were done in pen and ink and acrylic on masonite.
Design by Michael Solomon
Printed and bound in Malaysia